LAST PAWN SHOP IN NEW JERSEY

LAST PAWN SHOP
IN NEW JERSEY

POEMS

James Hoch

Louisiana State University Press

Baton Rouge

Published by Louisiana State University Press
lsupress.org

LSU Press Paperback Original

Designer: Laura Roubique Gleason
Typefaces: Adobe Jenson Pro, text; Cervo Neue, display

Cover photograph by Adonis Page, iStock Images

Library of Congress Cataloging-in-Publication Data

Names: Hoch, James, author.
Title: Last pawn shop in New Jersey : poems / James Hoch.
Description: Baton Rouge : Louisiana State University Press, [2022]
Identifiers: LCCN 2021022712 (print) | LCCN 2021022713 (ebook) | ISBN 978-0-8071-
    7405-0 (paperback) | ISBN 978-0-8071-7700-6 (pdf) | ISBN 978-0-8071-7701-3
    (epub)
Subjects: LCGFT: Poetry.
Classification: LCC PS3608.O27 L37 2022 (print) | LCC PS3608.O27 (ebook) |
    DDC 811/.6—dc23
LC record available at https://lccn.loc.gov/2021022712
LC ebook record available at https://lccn.loc.gov/2021022713

For my teachers, Michael Collier and Stanley Plumley

In memory of my mother, Doris McMath

Contents

LAST PAWN SHOP IN NEW JERSEY

Prayer for That Little Exhaustion of Light

There ought to be a prayer
for that little exhaustion of light
where bullets worm clear through
apples clinging to limbs.
There ought to be a prayer
for flesh they pass through,
space left, bits blown into grass,
that they resemble teeth,
and the grass taking teeth.
Look how sky eats report,
how skins of trees drink sound.
Prayer for saplings lined in rows,
winters we burlapped young trunks,
fed shovels of shit and ash.
The prayer ought to feel like hours
with the assassin of our orchard,
whose eyes are cold rain,
whose heart is cistern,
who has no use for prayer.
We know because we made him.
Because we made him, he is alive.
Who could blame us for wanting
a gauze to pack holes,
a god to backfill with breath?
Now a table in the mutilated orchard,
let us bow our heads over cider.
The prayer should be brief,
the way brief blows itself out.
The prayer will fail, always
between what language says
and does. Where prayer fails,
now mouths full of autumn,

now the leaf fury reddens.
Yes, we are scared. Yes, we tire
being afraid, pleading now
in that light, that damn light.

Dedication

This poem is to my son who I worry
into a misshapen form of worry.
And to worry itself, how it hangs
like a blanket over the head of a horse.
Why do they blanket the heads of horses
standing alone in a field, not seeing,
their skins seeking each other's aloneness?
I have no idea. I have never owned a horse,
though property is no giver of ideas.
Forgive me, my mother has died.
I am trying to understand, so my son
understands why his father's saying
nothing in the car, the yard, at the table.
My mother has died. Do you know?
It's like standing in a field,
then it's like the field being gone.
No one notices in the clumsy fog.
Do you see there is no distance?
She is not a thing. There are no figures
for this grief, the air tastes of ground.
Have you ever lost all context?
The other day, walking across the room,
my son looked at me like he was
eyeing a sick planet, then put his arms
around his weeping father,
as if holding a planet might heal it.
I want to thank him, but only have this poem,
a raft made from the skins of horses.
It is wrong he feels asked to wade.
His love just wants to rush out,
a busted hydrant a forever sunny day

Afghanistan

Somewhere inside my brother—
                 field of poppies,
brown river dragging brown land,

ragged mountains, miles of caves
                       wind-bored.

Stand still long enough, I hear
                 a boy with one leg
throwing stones at a boy with no legs,

because he takes pity, because he can.

Look harder, the body of a soldier
                 halved in the middle

of telling a joke, and another
snagging flies out of the air
                 in his sleep.

     And a goat wandering into a field.

Somewhere inside the goat
                 I've turned my brother into—

a few words for what he has done
             and silence

and a shrug when I try to say
what matters matters.

          And blood.

And bones
            which you have filled with sand
which time spills back.

And if I try to steady, fix,
            he'll say in his casual way

You don't know shit, as he hauls his body
along a hoof-marked ridge.

                    ⚞

Somewhere inside my brother
            —knock, wind opens him—

there are two skies: sky, sky of martins
                            returning to their boxes.

This is when I pray the choir of skies and birds
inside the goat that is the body of my brother

        conspire and lift him out of Afghanistan.
And Afghanistan becomes a cough I clear.

                    This is when I tire of making
my brother into some other,

            when the song of making becomes
the song of unmaking, the unsayable psalm,

            the one I've been telling myself
works him back into a man.

Disgrace and Oblivion in Ancient Rome

Sometimes names were shaved from relief,
chiseled off or written over with others'
scrawled with frenzied hammer. Sometimes
one man's head took another's ear; the image
mauled, contorted until nothing looked true.
Refiguring one thing for the aggrandizement
of another, it's older than the hills. All day I was
thinking it over—The morning Gabija was sick,
cross-legged in bed, eating a jar of horseradish,
I took her son, Pijus, for a walk in the park
outside Vilnius, where Soviets fashioned
the stone of Jewish cemeteries into Stalin.
When I think of Pijus, he looks like me,
or what my son might, bored, tracing the wells
of letters with his finger. Then he's running
toward me, hands cupped, lifting them to his ear.
In the dark, a cricket, a little song amid history.

My father, who taught history thirty-eight years
but drank longer and with greater dedication,
told me history was dust. It was noon, both of us
warm on chowder and cherryless manhattans.
He must've meant the dust of books, of stacks
of *Civil War Times*, dust of a lens, of a projector
he captained nodding off, dust of a warbling record,
dust of stone, of a slave's hand, of furnace,
dust of field, of horse dragging plow,
dust of work camp, death camp, breath,
dust of one tower, another coming down,
the birds disturbed seething in and out of form.
I have no idea what my father meant, or can't figure
how he held it together—history and liquor.

Once I saw a horse shot in the head. I was sitting
in the Cutlass beside my father. Ahead, a pickup's
flashers blinked in fog. The driver pulled a gun off
the window rack, stood over the buggy wrecked
on its side, the horse broken in its traces. Another
lifted the horse's head, held it awhile, in his lap.
I thought the man might fix the horse, its place
of dying. Instead, my father covered my eyes,
as if he could blind the clap spreading over
the field, the far ridge, the sky filling, the blood.
All my life I wanted his hands. Now, if I could,
I'd leave them for air, the way Pijus, who knew
a hundred ways to kill an insect, left the cricket
in the grass. And though they are not the same,
it is hard to say this world, the last, the other
we have yet to know are not the same, that a star's
brilliance and misery are not the same, that Pijus
is not the boy I was, that I am not the man he already is.

I was thinking about it walking near the newly
unveiled aqueducts, crabs scurrying white
in the video's bright flood. In Rome, still young,
my wife and I, holding hands as we crossed—
Gregorio, Claudia, Annia, Aurelio, Capo D'Africa.
And there, a man squatting against a wall,
a wad of newspaper in his hand. And there—
rising up, decaying down, the Colosseum
small, far off, distant-flat like a painting,
before the pocks of erosion, before the rosary
of coin and traffic, before ancient became kitsch.

Still time for the thing to stay, film at the end
of a film, screen white, reel aching in its circle,
the way Pijus and the cricket looked being held,
the way they do now—ash stepping out of
ashcan, memory the wind shifts into nothing.
I can't explain this. It goes on older than
the hills of Rome or Vilnius or New York.
Walking in a park, looking at things, it was brief.

Recess

There is a boy on the blacktop.
You must forget that, set him aside,
even when the ring of children,
merciless and unforgiving, tease him
for what he said about the new girl,
her clean dress blooming white
against her skin. *Pretty* is what he said.
And saying it out loud startled him
like a crocus on a morning walk
or a fish leaping out of a river.
The eye stills; the river refracts.
But do not think of what he said,
the sudden unhinged spritely urge,
or how he recanted or clarified
for a Black girl. You must think
instead of the girl so far away,
twenty steps away, in a circle
in a square, a ball calling out names
of her classmates. She is there;
a month later—an image floating
in a boy's head, beautiful head
open like a window, beautiful
window. Do not think *shame,*
the cruelty of going against one's own
instinct to love, how it festers—a seed
inside forty years until she appears again
as marginalia in a notebook: *Pretty
Black Girl, Third Grade—*
an image floating in a boy's head.
America: It is not easy, the stench
of sweat and hemp around the neck.
He wants you to know that. And that
it doesn't matter if he stands at a cliff
pointing at the dissolving figure of a girl,

you are looking at his finger,
you are breathing inside his speech,
beautiful finger, beautiful speech.
goddamn finger, goddamn speech.
He wants you to think only of her,
not pity, not envy how well he made
words change the order of things.

Gainer

Not Burke clutching groceries we smuggled
way late to the park where we conspired
to rendezvous as if spies or French.
Not rivulets of smoke caught under the pavilion,
as we gathered disbelieving, but not in disbelief,
a father could disown a son too good to be
condemned, even as the cops' spotlights
spoked his lean Frampton-headed shadow.
A kid about to run, pasty, shifty, a face
Caravaggio might paint—No, Blessed Comrades
of Perpetual Yearning, I, Carny of Delinquent
and Mustered Earnestness, present *Burke*
skinny but tough in cut-offs, steadying himself
on the springboard at the town pool,
as we cloyed in gutters, watching him pound
tuck tumble turn toward away held aloft,
nailing a reverse one and a half gainer.
Ridiculous—the way he entered water,
as if the water already knew he was coming.
And the strangeness—not perfection,
that he'd rise through the turbulent cloud,
breach our mirrored faces, and be perfect again,
like he was born for it, the sharp lamp
promise of this moment being fixed. Surely
this, if nothing else, would never leave.
In time, like time, we move wayward,
one inconceivable world into another,
forward backward all at once. *Sweet. Wasted.*
I yell at the video of kids taking pleasure
injuring themselves—leaping off a neighbor's roof,
landing in slapdash pools. Then say *Don't.*
Don't confuse the nature of beauty for whim,
and lecture on the shape of Benjamin's dream
parataxis, recursivity and *crow crow crow* . . .

Attention: Punk Minstrels and Vagrant Youth,
you who wear Burke's face around the mall,
like a cast party of the dead, like it's all one thing—
claims are the least thing we make
fleeing this life, if that is what we do,
as we torque our tongues, lie our faces off,
a story practiced, so well-versed
we become the understudies of our bodies.

Pine Barrens

So what if fascinated with a Zippo's
    flint and glint, flick and click,
        a fondness for accelerants,
we lit a few trees ablaze. So what if
    we left a few of us behind drying out

from a stew of booze and Percocet
    lifted from Scully's cabinet,
        where else could we have
welcomed such plunderings—iron dank
    cedar ponds and yellow roads

meandering through thick black pine,
    scrub oak as dark and thorny
        and *Blair Witch Project* as one gets
in the wilds of South Jersey—
    where all prank and crank we blew

our bodies lunar and fed our selves
    open sky, a loon's paltry cry, its song,
        the instrument of longing,
the place of displacement, transmogrifying,
    absurd—we fed it everything;

it took it. And yeah smoked, dropped
    and laid on the hood of a '66 Ford Galaxy,
        we let the moon paint through
smelter plume, smudged in burnt needle,
    in marrow of bones split by blue flame.

In the bongy rafters of nostalgia
    what shall we say we saw

when we cured wonder,
our bodies a low bog of ransacked joy,
    where hithering hurt begot salve,

before we dragged ourselves home
        and plummeted back into the work
            of being where we came from?
How shall we call the orphaned self,
    the one being devoured,

what we took for pleasure?
        Friends, it's been way too long.
            Find me again, stacking
our pacts and dreams like kindling
    in those body-strewn woods.

You will know my ragged smell,
        slouchy in the paunch,
            singing the song of keep singing,
the meaning of touch more touch,
        the meaning of mouth more mouth.

Self-Portrait as Last Pawn Shop in New Jersey

Lately I have not been feeling myself.
I walk around like a figure missing
its ground. I see a braid of smoke
a hand passes through and envy hands,
how smoke stays on skin, the faint
hairs of a cheek a hand brushes against.
Used to be enough to be the blown engine
of a VW outside of Durango, whiskey
we killed watching our father die, a bad
painting I loved because our mother
loved bad paintings, without irony.
Lead sinkers in the gray bay of self—
There! I'd say, strapped to the mast
of a tall ship in a Turner painting,
or a grip dangling from the center pole
of a circus tent above a troupe of dachshunds
trying to find the tiny pedals of tricycles.
I collected myself like I was vying to be
the last pawn shop in New Jersey.
Now I am not even a whir of gnats
on a dirt road, a threadbare cloud
on a ridgeline, the steam riding off
an old man stepping out of a sauna.
Days nothing seems to tie me to me.
The more I live, the more the rucksack
lightens, the more I can't find myself
in the mirror of the world, and roam
storefronts as if I have misplaced myself.
When I was a kid, I used to keep
a Pringles can filled with volcano rocks
someone once sold as Apache Tears,
one weird ass way of marketing pain.
Gone now, as the name of the boy
I bailed out for stealing CDs from Walmart,

for the girl he crushed on. Which is not
really a crime I explained to the cops.
The girl loved Stevie Nicks so much
I found her stoned under blackberry bramble,
listening to "Landslide" on a Walkman.
Perhaps it matters to say they were Apache or
Pueblo, Inde or Kewa, that they were
minor thieves flung far from home.
Perhaps all they wanted was the ground
inside each other. But even as I say
Landslide, Walkman, I feel the scree
of words, the pawn shop emptying out.
The things that made me are ether now,
as clear as those who went and died
and took what mattered—bodies, a joke,
a late meal that wove itself into morning—
as if they had packed for the afterlife.
And empty and whole and empty,
the air inside me tastes like leaving,
and leaving tastes like rain that never comes.
Which I love like breath on a window,
like someone else drawing a heart, a face
a pleasure in the taking. No wonder,
I am marveling over the demo crew
slaying each other: *Fuck wad, lug nut,*
waste of skin—Cuts, we used to call them,
nicking wing, heel, gutting into laughter,
then, tender tender, as one with angels
or dogs, where the wound is transom.
The words hold them to the ground,
and I am whatever hovers when they go.

Poem at the End of a Pier

Ripped, rippling in sun, slack lacquered glaze,
water and sky all pooling slate and abiding—
a pair of boys at the end of a pier, shirtless
bravado of baggy jeans and flagging boxers,
defined yet not, not yet too much like men,
drawing wrist rockets arched Arcadian
slinging Alka-Seltzer into a horde of gulls
that dive veer ascend, then recompose chaotic
plural in their orchestration. And if not for trick
bikes skateboards self-conscious colors,
you'd think a scene thugged from another age
flowing back, chimeric, alchemic, so marvel
over their punk-stature alive cut like horses
poised above the surf's edge at the Steel Pier
ready to leap, and the crowd leaning against
the rail, the ocean not spectacle enough.
Or, 1943—soldiers boarding a troop carrier
parading down gray smoking Manhattan,
the harbor gaping and farther the open Atlantic,
and women night-shifting the paper factory,
bleach-blistered skin, tainted lung reed-slick
cracked like the sick femur of a heron.
What do the boys know of where they are?
What do you know of their lack of eyes
clouded like clayed apples on an orchard floor?
They are what they are, what you see;
and the cleft silence between pooling,
as they ride back up the kill road toward
oranging garages of shears and kerosene,
never leaving after-swirl of river ocean,
gravity tide, bracken core, estuarial roil
palette and swill of the Hudson—Half Moon,

Dutch Colonial, General Electric, Indian Point—
mastic pastoral washed in resin, vehicle.
O soul, hungry, hungered, what you've come to,
flux and thrum, a mask to say the world through.

II

This Drink Tastes Like History

April, Richmond, a scattering of blossoms,
horse chestnuts over the Confederate lawn,

a memory of snow, and the bloom-gone
tweeking limbs shot thin as charcoal drawings of

one-way junkies stepping off a Greyhound bus—
I imagine Levis thinking something like that,

Etch-A-Sketching his mind as the bartender
at The Hill Café pours a round just after noon,

his body a hotel crammed long strung-out
toomuchness, edgy in the purgatory of a score.

Nowhere near 1996, it is now, and now is
irrecoverable as a wave, as this drink,

which sends me into history, a field
outside a barn gig to empty out under stars.

The band's covering Bowie, so in my head
I am ten, skinny, boardwalk strutting along

the Steel Pier in Atlantic City. High above
on a platform, a woman wearing a swimsuit

and football helmet sits bareback on a horse,
waiting to coax unnatural into real.

The first "Diving Girl" was named Sonora.
She went blind from hitting the water wrong

and kept diving another eleven years. That's why
this one is wearing aviator goggles. That the helmet's

leather, no face mask, the kind my father wore
playing nose guard, a detail that indicts the detailer.

It's a good day to muck around the mid-70's,
my father standing beside me, a relic—Polo shirt,

buzz cut, most of his teeth lost to a field of men,
sweating manhattans, whiskey sours. A good

drinker, almost everyone loved his commitment.
Not my mother, who just leapt out of marriage;

which, if this were a script, you would already know.
The idea of Atlantic City was to become dream,

aspire toward another world. The way, in a field
Levis and my father alive, hovering, I disappear

in the wake of my breathing. It works a bit, a spell,
a hit off a pipe in a dive bathroom. In the end

the woman and horse land in a pool and my father
says, *Now that's a broad.* In the end my father

wasted his material. I am now the age he was then,
the age Levis was in '96, and the man who tended

bar at The Hill Café is the same man serving drinks.
Small world. And symmetry being occasion,

but I get confused speaking across decades.
They drift into each other, snow across a road.

Remember the snow? Reader, can I call you Reader?
Have we hung enough we can let go formalities

of distance? Did you skid home, get snowed in, like me,
with a woman whose voice could fill and sink you?

When she sang it felt like a first listening,
like she was returning it to purity. Days later,

the plow showed, and she became a painting,
a landscape she invited me to walk out of.

Or maybe I simply bored her and she left.
Sometimes I hear her on the radio and think *snow*

then *blessed*. One storm, slow-mo spectacle.
All this happened in 1996. Impossible: my father,

a woman I knew through accident of weather,
and Levis fidgeting, politely enduring company.

And just when they dissolve into each other,
Levis leans across the bar of this dream and says:

You are telling this for a reason. And maybe
you should stop turning women into paintings.

Some nights my life unspools like cans of 8 mm
spilling off the shelf of the sky, and I am making it here

in the dark, hands and a story of hands, trying
the buttons of my trousers in a field where I leave

the whole shit show, and let the field resolve.
Once I am almost gone, what love becomes emptiness?

Walking away, calling back—low whistle,
recurring wind, snow shifting across a road,

a song the band's way inside, another round.
White, the horse was white, a mare; as in

monster, foolish woman, the sea. Somehow
it matters, depending on what you mean.

Landscape Resembling My Mother Dying

It was the deer that drew me, the rub of red
brash through brown in a field of ragged
saplings, stray forsythia, white crowns of lace,
behind the barbed wire and chainlink fence
of the Marathon Battery superfund site.
It was still, or nearly still, feeding amid
legislation in the not-field, not-meadowed
lot, and deadpanned back my stupid gaze.
I had been drinking with a friend. No,
that's not quite right. He was watching me
drink, as I rambled on about Edgerton's
strobe photography. Who would spend a life
trying to capture a drop of milk? *Freud,*
my friend said, then screwed up his face.
You are not really asking, are you? No clue
and no idea what the deer wanted, though
it seemed to say: *Dude, draw.* I mean
sketch this flowering in the marginalia
of the Chinese takeout menu. I admit now
I am as far from understanding deer
as watching drops of milk fall, but stood there
waiting for the influence in such moments.
No dice. And, yeah, the midday beer,
but I swear the deer wanted this too,
like she was doing me a pastoral solid,
like she would've stayed in the swill
and debris of last century's science,
until streetlights and the stars' white brush
broke us into a Brooklyn sublime.
It didn't happen. The deer bolted clear,
and all I got was a snaggle of goldenrod
and hoof-struck sumac. But who cares?
Who knows if the deer lived through winter
or passed rush hour, vulture and crow

carrying cadmium home to messes of young?
I love my friend, how, after a lecture
on strobography, he returned me to the land
of no bullshit. When I got up to leave the bar,
he said *how is your mother?* I didn't say
the last time I saw her I leaned over her bed
and asked if I could take her picture,
that she said something I couldn't quite hear,
that I took the pic anyway. I remember thinking
I could say to him: *See, this is the last picture
of my mother alive.* That would've been unkind,
like expecting the deer to pose forever.
Dying is all I said, and told myself to sit
and draw her face, as it was before it went.
Don't ask. Don't ask where I get this,
this want to be drawn, captured, disappeared,
even if all we end with is a vague fragment
of a landscape we see but fear to breathe,
thumbing the mind for that word that means
something resembling milk. Maybe, it will return
when I lie down in bed and imagine my mother,
deer leaping into wood, slow burn, crash.
Maybe it will. And I will leave it at that.

Elegy with a Landscape of Iceland by Georg Guðni

Some days lay out like a dark suit on a bed
as if we get to choose what to live for.
Some days feel like you are in Iceland,
just off the road heading toward Silfra,
the moss-covered lava field and sky,
a smoky bay dissolving into itself.
You could be forgiven if you feel confused
that this is not Iceland, that you are only
looking at a painting you almost walk into.
Our eyes acclimate our body toward seeing,
so that as you move toward horizon line
this way of seeing is a talking in your head.
I had a friend once who, when first meeting
someone, used to ask: *What are you into?*
You could answer: bands, art, drugs, books,
but really he meant: *Man, how into it are you?*
He had a gift for making you feel fogged
enough you could be mistaken for a field,
that it was kind to be a landscape.
My friend was into cooking, which means
hungry all the time, which means the day
he collapsed from an overfed heart,
on the kitchen floor, middle of the night,
he was the happiest man I knew,
and there was no distance between who I was
and losing him. It's hard to explain.
You see, I am trying to find my way through,
as if this suit gets me to the other side of into,
beyond figure and ground, beyond divergence,
so that moving in and out of my own seeing
becomes a way of loving moss sky both rain.
It's like Iceland or Guðni's paintings
if your body has never been converted into
emptiness, then, holding, fills with water.

When his daughter spoke at my friend's funeral,
I could hear his syntax and wanted to claim
some acre of certainty. But I'd have to forgive
all the *ors* and *likes*. I'd have to overlook
flawed valve, cracked hinge, cold forehead.
Even this sentence hovers above something
that is not a sentence. Truth is: I am feeling
my age, and my age is wading through
the rain of my losses. A few days after he died,
we ate the meal he cooked that night,
and I thought goneness stays in the mouth.
It felt like setting hunger down, then
his daughter asked: *You still going to Iceland?*
And I remembered Silfra, it is real,
and if you are into it, and enter the water,
you'll need to don some gear. That cold
could stop your heart, and so damn clear
you can see as far as you can see. *Y'know man,*
you should, she said. *He would've dug that.*

Elegy with Icarus and the Heart of a Hummingbird

Someone must've gone and fetched him out,
towed the drowned, wing-wrecked bird
through a slick of his own feathery want,
though, more likely, he passed out
from knowing the falling distance
turns the surface hard on his body.
It must've mattered to his father, who
had to watch fishermen circle his son,
as if there was some meaning in water.
Is this any way to treat ones who wash ashore,
prodding with toe, stick, disbelieving finger?
This morning, walking along the road,
I found a hummingbird against the curb,
marveled at the glasswork of its stillness,
how the light was falling too, so I could
see shifting green and blue, the tiny cage,
the dark needle of its bill, the dark eyes
the ants will carry away. I can't say
if it died from wanting too much
or from finding what it wanted too much.
Surely, Icarus had the heart of a hummingbird.
If they revived him, would he have risen
back into the sky, damaged wiser,
or, bratty, simply blamed his crap wings?
I nudged the bird with my shoe, not expecting,
but half wishing a startling burst
through our myth-brightened world.
But the boy who ODed in a port-a-potty
was no bird at all. When his father found him,
his sun-jonesing heart large from hovering,
his friends, junk-caked booze-skanked
themselves, turned away, puked in a ditch,
praying he'd break the surface of his misery.
Even outside the funeral home, heavy coats

blocks long, suits they last wore at graduation,
dragging for some sliver of rachis and vane
jutting out where their wings might be,
they do not want to die, they only want
to feel less, less this. The way we too
curse all this away, we who love those
who love the air, the sudden lift and veer.

Palouse

Banking out of cloud bank—light, the upflung
startlingly bright onslaught, staggering
shock of verge, rush and roar, aloft, aloft
the veering whir teetering keeled off brink—
then, as sudden, an empty buoyant calm,
low cool draft whalelike and breathing again,
undulating miles of fields gently
deepening one another—a March green
quiet, spring on spring, early hum, turning,
sprawling over grasses of winter wheat—

of hue, a thing, yes and what a thing says
of a body racked and loved, of voice,
both borne—we tinker among, as verdant
as swaths pouring a skin shifting and thin
an eye barely holds its marvel—*too much,*
too much says grouch spit, says iron scorn,
and yet we mourn the not giving over,
even as color becomes sky, the sky
chromatic enough, and offer a song
lit and wavering as anything new

and clumsy as joy breaching the grief years.
Friend, one way to say this: *I am happy*
to see you, another: *Sorry about*
your mother—though death is not *about,*
muddles with us as we fall out of clouds
or enter the rooms of the dying, hands
in pockets, half expecting to fashion
a thing, make by unmaking, undo
the simple veil the practiced mask lifts
and the dark beneath becomes surface—thus

a song, as when you say *Good morning, Ma*
and she says *Ah Pinocchio,* staring
out a window, though there's no way to tell
if she's cracking a joke or if Jim Dine
left one dismembered outside a foundry
absurd like a patient oddly earnest
waiting to be welded. Hapless, *Morning*
you try again, as if trying could change
a thing. And this is how the gods know us,
our mouths agape, salt taking salt, singing.

Field songs of theft or stories the shape
of theft: a girl whose body turns commerce
because she gave her word to the grass,
because she could not have done otherwise:
a boy whose body became an offer
because the ocean would not be appeased:
the nerve-frayed hands of workers heading in
and out of trailers, sickly boxes
metal flecks scattered over the Palouse:
because even the word is dispossessed—

as origin, as swarm and cloud, the air
quivers into and through, of and toward,
ours its somehow here somehow beneath
the ascribed, beneath combine and bale,
yoke and hoofmark, beneath slope mound hollow,
beneath bunch june fescue, dark yards of silt-
lined basalt outwash wind-blown wind-crafted
augured in the blank bowl stillness of now—
breath before breath, body within body,
ovarian all now a killing field.

Still time for cocktails, your dying mother's
poor jokes—*have you heard the one about X*—
clutch of figs and cheese, some vague parts of duck,
an oaky white with a humdrum finish,
time to while away an hour in a book
about how to see what not to breathe,
dozing off, a head resting down dreamless
against another, let it take you in
and not worry what plague, what coming dark
slowly fills the body like a black bath.

Unto water—among dead, wading, bent
close and kneeling so that our faces rise
mirroring back their own, so that held
we hold too the children they once were,
that ours are arms of boys we used to be—
unto water, unto grass, fold on fold
we lay down in their dying, they kiss us
with our words and we curse back with theirs
and see in their still-open eyes our heads
slathered astonished shimmering. Heavy

heavy this quarry sack of all we have,
heavy heavy this disease of forgetting,
heavy accrual, the plaquing rivers
that leave us chalk-white, wandering blighted
unreturned ankle-deep in the shallows—
heaving we lug our flooded selves toward
flickering surface quickening wick oiled
cetaceous flaring into flame, falling
ancient, true as tumor as harvest blade
burning us away after some other

when we wheel strung in this deluge
gut-raw singing beyond wow, beyond cure,
beyond scape and scree of what we want
or grieve, toward no distance, no kind,
the bright hour when wind does not act,
aubade and elegy commune collapse,
where the grass sounds and rises to meet us
where we flour our bodies in its ash
and listening down say *it is* as fire
it is, it is as a green quiet forms.

Puberty with Self-Portrait as Tiffky Doofky

Just the sound, like some fingery
instrument flourishing in a symphony,
like a sixteenth-century woodwind favored
by Corsicans. Or, as a friend says,
more like a dog being shot into space,
lonely, irretrievable—Dear Boy,
buoyant in the sea of your own biology,
I'm trying. In the naming of metaphor
I'm as lost as you. If it were a film,
Invasion of the Body Snatchers, after
the larvae hatch beneath your skin.
Apt, almost everyone survives, plus
you learn to live a little more gamey.
I know this comes from the annals
of the dashed and unvarnished,
but if it comforts to have some thing
to carry you through, I will dumpster-
dive the diner ruin of my pubescence
which handily sounds like has-no-sense.
What's that? *Some knowledge is power.*
Some just gross. And the video the nurse
has gathered you discreetly together
to watch in a darkened room, the one
requiring my signature, will leave you
dumbstruck as a monk walking
out of a seminary, educed beyond
whatever the mind wanted to hold,
listening so devoutly inside the body's
tremor and hum he does not hear the dogs
barking at the window, until stepping off
the bus, into the driveway, he wakes
from a sleep that was anything but sleep.
I am sorry to say you will feel like this.
I am sorry I am no fortune-teller,

cast no spell, no armor to dip you in.
I love too much to lie. You will see me,
the garbage collector, riding a tractor
through the village streets, a wagon
the children chase after, trying to fill
with the heads of daisies. Confused,
you want to claim me, but the children
sing loudly a song about a goat farmer
who was sacrificed to the god of milk.
You shy your body away and let go.
You want me to wait on the other side,
distance an offering, and I want to make
your offering a house anarchists burn
to a field of singed and smoldering sugar.
Our clothes, our hair, the sweet smoke
to ward off the dark, to bring luck—
I kiss you on the forehead,
strike an iron ring with an iron rod,
the clang of language, the ocean nag
of my kisses pulling you back
from wherever your body is taking you.

Halo

On the X-ray I could see the fracture,
the shadow veining through the ghost
of the vertebra he cracked playing
football, hard-nosed in the driveway
because it was Sunday, and Sunday
means church and football in America,
even if you are Yaqui. And because
he was Yaqui he played and prayed
to the tattoo of Santa Teresa scrolled
up his forearm. And because my job,
the legal guardian of the group home,
and had the power over matters his
—school, work, body—I signed for
the halo brace they screwed into his skull,
one needle at a time to deaden nerves,
one pin at a time to restrict mobility,
each entering a dissent I cringed with.
And because I was from New Jersey,
white enough, educated sort of
I qualified to hold his hand each turn
the wrench made, each tear not shed,
never never cry in front of a white man.
And I held his hand, the one that killed
a man in Tucson in a fight he didn't ask for,
but killed the man anyway, with a knife
in the street, a detail I knew but forgot
as I forgot all the crimes of those kids
my boss called my *charges*, because
I could, and forgetting is privilege.
The way I forgot to tell the boss I too
had a record, a fact I quietly expunged,
because whiteness affords slippage.
Lord knows, nothing bespeaks the redress
of genocide and systemic brutality

like sending a white boy from Jersey
to tighten a spiral, to close the loops
in his cursive, a kid not much older
than the one gripping my hand because
I was there, on duty, because he asked me
to stay with him when they set the halo in
like an angel I said, *like a deer head*
he said, because Pascua Yaqui dancers
strap the heads of deer to their own
heads, because Sonora, because Yaqui,
and the heads of deer and heads of Yaqui
are *not like* but *of.* And because the border
of the reservation is white on one side,
rez on the other, they promised no pain,
they promised fear and fixed his head
to see only forward as if pinning him
to the ground to stare at an eclipse.
And because I am no tourist to suffering,
I gave no tears. And because he asked,
and the landscape of feeling is my song,
I waited for him to fade into the midday
night of codeine. Then wept, wept white,
in the corridor, the parking lot, looping
into a gray cloud as I drove back home
to other kids, who said nothing about
the ghost I was wearing on my face,
the song I hardly deserve to call my own,
if it is mine or his, this house, this country,
wherever we are, we have come to.

Sunflowers

Standing in front of Van Gogh's portrait,
the winter one, bandaged, heavy green
overcoat, blue hat black fur, each stroke
deft, pained as the face he is showing,
mangled but repairing as if lived through,
something worth pleading on canvas—
my son asks *What happened to his head?*
He's still a kid and doesn't know the story,
the unbearability of loving ones who leave.
When I don't answer he eats the quiet,
the way when I turn down the radio's litany
of casualties, he hunkers like a monk
burying his head in a bowl of Cheerios.
But really, what is there to say—
a photo, my brother patrolling a field
of sunflowers in Afghanistan. It'll be years
before he understands the ear, that presence
implicates the missing. It'll be just after
school lets out, driving to the grocery store,
and he will tell me about another Van Gogh,
a vase of sunflowers studied in art class.
Simple task: To record how each differs,
this head from that, this paint from that.
We will be crossing the creek bridge
and he will be mid-sentence and I will be
thinking summer—roadsides lined with flowers
in black buckets, and birds taking seed
out of ones along the garden fence,
wondering if he knows about Gauguin,
the Yellow House in Arles. And just
when I feel almost useful, he will ask:
Did your brother have to kill anyone?
What I don't know becomes signature.
What I can't say becomes silence

and silence scores the mind, and the mind,
never letting go, takes the marks and makes
a house of the cuttings, and the house says,
dwell here. But all that's outside the frame.
We are here now, looking backward
and forward at a painting of a man
injured in love. And if I had the means,
I'd ditch the day, turn all elsewheres noise,
and hold truant the coma calm of a museum.
And if I had the heart not to feel this forever's
not the one my son wants, I'd break it,
strew it against the bric-a-brac and static.
To stay still this long is a terrible thing to ask.

Global Studies

Where the hell are we you wonder
when you've spent the night meandering
the blind alleys of some ancient city
where you wake vertiginous, not knowing
what *where* means, let alone the *you*
you left in the streets. It's an old scene
playing on the television—a man
just after dawn lingers at the railing
of a hotel balcony overlooking a piazza.
And when the shot demands a profile,
the camera pans, turns the protagonist
a wee urny, the sudden sea behind him.
Beautiful toomuchness is one way of
describing the cinema of the midcentury,
though one could say the same for early
cartography. Is this lost on you, alien?
Are you lost in a volute of talking?
I am speaking to you, little dung head
etching the silo cell of a milk glass.
You don't seem to worry your home;
lethal, though, to not know how it works,
how this glass was once some earth.
Yes you, lover of filth, draining the simple
thing you need, *This is no way to live,*
I shout from my manufactured shore.
It's me, your scorn-loving eye-baller.
There's Rome, Bilbao, Secaucus,
the semiotics of dying. But you shrug
in your bug shruggery way, stuck-in,
seeing-through, trying to skirt under
the heavy rim, dreaming scat and sun.
Even in your dream, shrewd whim,
a field of entry and decay pranked

with random one-way signs,
I want nothing more than to trespass
in the mucky regulars, and nothing
you want more than to traverse the face
of a world that will not let you be.

Lithium Bath

In Mexico, idling in a taxi, watching
a thin man hunched over a slab
being swallowed by stone billowing
from his circular blade, as he cuts
and fits perfect tiles so well-heeled
patrons of Hotel Colonia won't turn
an ankle strolling the cobbled lane—
It is easy to think transubstantiation
is a form of forgetting. Christ even,
even at death, tried to be forgotten into
some other, and if he was left alone
surely would've turned into fine slivers,
the way stone forgets heavy, and the man,
who seems just a few years older than
the boy he was, forgets the air he breathes
was once the silt of a sea settling now.
Where did the boy go? Who tailed
his father like a pup working for scraps
of affection, who a school friend
once leaned over a bottle and kissed
with all the conscious tenderness
reserved for string-tied letters.
Mostly now, he is cloud, a sketch
barely visible, except the faint pulse of
a red bandanna he uses for a mask.
If I could retrieve the boy from the fog
and pull him back into the foreground
of his body, if I could resist like a heart
trite comparisons, if I could make
a world less like grinding a man into
the shape of whim or common desire,
if he would forgive this intrusion,
it would feel like a bath to float and drift
blessed long enough in lithium his body,

its strata of hurt and kisses, would forget
it is a body, until even his father might
look on him rising out of dust, water, day,
and take him for the small peach he once
was born as is has been always becoming.

Advice to a Son as Garden Statuary

I am not sure you understand
       what I am saying regarding ticks,
about mice and voles being more
          ridden than elegant yard-strewn deer
      sporting that stupid you-don't-see-me pose.

Just because one bears a name
       doesn't mean one belongs forever.
Also, wearing underwear on your head to school
         will so haunt thy days. Pay attention to Keats,
      who knew some things about disease

and statues. Left alone long enough,
       they harden. Ask your crap dad, his hands
trafficking air, his rage vein filling
         like a levee with the blood memory
      of a failure he's trying to overcome.

When he loses his shit, he believes
       something more solid grows inside you
and heavy since you were born
         that he's carried bed unto bed,
      drinking the good sweet smell.

I don't know what's more laughable:
       faith in certainty, or certainty in faith—
The light disbelieving deer, or stone-still you
         staring blank-faced on the lawn
      watching your father's love turn him weird.

I don't know a lot of things, least of all
       how to live without casualty.

I come from a long line of cagey smirkers
          lurching toward reckless affection.
     Stunning, the valley between what you expect

and what his ridiculous heart delivers.
          One day: Molokai. The next: Korengal.
Mostly: stuttering hug and shrug.
          If you could hover above
          the daily topiary in one of those Lego

helicopters, you would see the beauty
          of this fail, how it goes way beyond taste
or trust. Seriously, it would make you weep,
          as if seeing brought conviction.
     Do you remember that kind of weeping?

Polycardial

You don't have to be a cephalopod
to understand it's good to have a spare
hidden somewhere in the body's crags.
You don't need to possess random
superpowers nor free dive in arctic rifts
or play emotional whack-a-mole.
I mean, who couldn't use a wonderfully
engorged backup, a blue reliever
to answer the hunger of being human.
You never know. You never know.
But spares, these days, hard to come by.
Can't score them in the East Village
anymore, not dozing on a bench
in Tompkins Square Park, not even
Brooklyn. Forget Brooklyn. Imagine.
Some days you slump in the paunch
of a lawn chair, sipping gin and tonic,
and a Gremlin goes by and you dream
the smell of your teenage self and herself,
how you took time, how she showed you,
kissing in an orange beater that forever
faintly stunk of oil and singed carburetor
hose and stale Parliament cigarettes.
Her car, her mouth. It was good, right?
In your rush, you were kind, right?
All those fantasies are now memories.
They float in a softly lit aquarium
exhibit you've curated your whole life,
and you are almost returned to 1982
yellowy streetlamp night, cassettes
playing "Take on Me" . . . "I Melt with You" . . .
Why are we equal parts tender and not?
Perhaps, we were once polycardial:
one heart of air; the other air that burns.

Maybe one burst and cauterized
the other. Or the humans exhausted
all the feelings, so ran to the fjord
and threw our wasted heart into the sea.
Which might explain squid and octopi,
and why we are lousy at swimming,
and why your heart thaws in the sink
of your old tired weak worn-out body
which no longer sleeps, which wakes
and stirs the warm second you hear
your wife open the screen door
or children shrieking in the yard
as they gather jarfuls of fireflies.
Listen: Let the air be an ocean.
Let the ocean occupy your tongue.

The Ask

13 and trembling, sequestered in your room,
you undo a square of paper a girl named Becky
folded over and over, a sweat-damp compression
in which you feel the torque of a life coming,
a frantic hand trying to get the ask down
before it is forever gone: You + Me = Dance?
An equation that is a question, you decipher
ambiguity in math, certain as certain can be
someone else exists on the other side of words.
A girl, a real one, kind and breathing, sees
pleasure in algebra, shivery alive with it.
Ain't it like waking, ladybugs hundreds
swarming the walls, windows, space light takes?
13 and already Borges—world constructed,
we act like hands have done none of the labor.
Your father, never more useless, who appears
extraterrestrial in and out of your doorway,
only wanting to talk about flux, the universe,
wishes he could say your skin is not a wall,
infestations get easy. Instead, he says, *steady*,
as if wired to a bomb he's charged with disarming.
You have no language for the alien who believes
advice matters, who thinks he can talk himself
out of being the alien you turned him into.
He doesn't get it. Even this poem wants to hurl
him back to whatever planet evicted him.
So you only muster *Leave? Please?* making
an imperative out of a question. Forgive
his stupid grin, his loitering, his forgetting.
It will be like this, he won't say, in a few years,
cancer or some such, as it was when his father
turned and could not say who he was seeing.
There is no reason to remind you how brief it is,
how the river asked Heraclitus to wade,

and in his half-ass way, in time's cold wake,
he started to sing a broken held-together song.
No, you don't need to know about Heraclitus,
ento- or ety-mology, your father's weirdness.
None of this. You are only 13, unfolding
a piece of paper, word by word, the scrawling,
your body an origin room busy with wings.

Leaving Well Enough Alone

In the dream of my death it is snowing,
my mother and father are together, happy,
I think, like they've let go a sharp thing
and frolic in the snowy kingdom of my death.
When they were alive, it took a few drinks
for this want for life. Then not at all. Okay,
wool coats, cartoon mittens, laughter—
leave well enough alone, I tell my dead self.
The snow is like a bed we once piled on,
a photograph I saw and marveled over,
as if it walked out of nothing and got lost.
The way dreams dissolve just as the artifice
of dreams appear, just as my orphan self steps
out of snow and puts his hand on my shoulder.
My orphan self never wears a shirt, so I see
the photo tattooed in the center of his chest.
All my life I've confused a hand calming me
with a hand waking me. This woman
lying beside me nudges against my sleep,
as she falls back into her own dream.
I have no idea what she is dreaming,
though I've loved her for years, her scent
lays my orphan self down in a bath.
I want to say somewhere inside her
there's a joy made of water. I want to wake
and tell her, like I've discovered something.
Do you see how I am always the orphan boy
waiting for the sure hand of togetherness?
I want to ask if she's okay that my parents
suffer in our bed, that the god of consent
grants us our being. But it's taken years
to learn how to let her be, how to take off

my clothes in the always falling snow
and let sleep have us, this country of
tongues and palms and mouths open to sky.

Parking Garage

In the end you have to go home.
You have to leave the hospital room

where you stand bedside, though
there's no bed anymore, which

an hour ago was hers. In the end
nothing belonging to no body,

hers no longer hers, you must head
down the ramp, through the sliding

glass doors and cheap fluorescence
of a gray garage, and find the car

she parked somewhere weeks ago.
Which level? Which space?

You ask someone in scrubs for help,
and she can see you are not right

and gentle with your notrightness.
You are saying nothing new.

You are a son; your mother has died.
All you need to do is find the car.

But you can't even, and break again—
It will be this way awhile:

Driving down the turnpike, tired of
feeling rented, chemo urine talc

stubborn in the leather, you tell yourself
your body needs to be yours again—

Then relief, guilt, a profusion.
But all that's fiction,

a person you have yet to be.
Right now, grief is simple: Find the car,

let the engine run some, take care
not to damage anything on the way out.

Primitivo Negativo

We are out of wine. And that's a problem
in Puglia or Pittsburgh. Watman's got
a seawater risotto he's feeding dandelions
and periwinkles, and the totemic look
of the Pacific Northwest—ocean facing,
as if he's sending monsters back to the deep.
Skoog's picking a Stanley Brothers tune
about sinfulness on the banjo while waiting
for okra in a gumbo to break just right.
He's singing about the hills of Virginia
but somehow predictably the flotsam of
Bywater and Katrina floats in the verses,
when Genoways shows up, a wild boar
tied to the bed of his pickup. *The only
sustainable operation in the Poconos,*
but stinks like frack sluice. We've been
going since late morning and the day's
rolled geologically along, our loved ones
scattered on the periphery of the yard
because evening feels immortal and ours.
We love them enough to forage from keel
and underbrush as we ply one another
with jars and stories about some others
sitting around a fire, songs as good as ours.
Not true, of course. But we are out of wine
and someone needs to make a run, scavenge
the deli for underwhelming but drinkable.
Stay close to God you might hear before
heading down mountain, where you count
car-bludgeoned trees. Won't be me; my dream.
Why should I get out of my boxers?
Why should any of us answer the warrant?
No one will wander farther than earshot:
So we can holler and laugh and grow

serious regarding missed cheese,
corked wine, a goat being lovingly
slaughtered in the yard, if love and brevity
and mercy are delivered workmanlike.
There are facts not to tinker out of:
Tar sands. War. Water. . . . We know this,
though we've never been in the same room
together, just figures floating in ether.
Stay close to God. No one's really a believer,
but we believe what wine says to glass,
knife to block, shank and catgut and rafters,
the body's comings and goings, prayers
that return friends wonky but whole.
Let us loll our heads to the clonky gods
of togetherness, simple pleasures laid out
on a table that was once a door opening
and closing a life of alibis and sentences.

Small Orange

Someone harried must've dropped it,
quietly lost it from bag to sidewalk
where it lolled to a still like midday.
Some passerby must've thought:
Cool. Small sun. I got this.
Then placed it, just so, on the curb
as if he was Yoko Ono or some other
artist with lots of Os in her name.
No wonder the photographer from
Orlando took time with the orange
alchemically debulking all context
so only orange floating in an orange
filmic bath and the eye orange
peers back in. That's a lot of orange,
urgent like a knock at an odd hour,
a woman disheveled on the porch,
perhaps car trouble or fleeing a rage.
Wait, wait: one voice says. Another:
Bow down. You've got this. . . .
Where there's story, there's craving—
You can't get that out of your head:
an equation, a rattle made from the shell
of a turtle. It wakes you, this simple
orange set before you in your dream
slowly making its way out of sleep.
What does it want? What will want do?
You've been taking it apart all day
wedge after wedge on a park bench,
feeding sparrows what you won't have.
Everything living says stays with you,
the way a body carries old light.
And you, bucket of worry and good,

will tender, will let the moment go,
until your tinkered machine picks up:
This is where we are. Love the cold.

The Listening

Snow again, I can't hear it falling
in birches, yard, garden beds, heady
tufts and root down of winter carrots,
though I stare out there, as if
listening to the making. The way,
a kid, I'd rise in the middle of night
looking for my father, the house
the usual dark I'd sleepwalk through.
Eventually someone would find me
sitting on the living room floor,
W-sitting, snow on television, or
staring canvas-blank out a window.
Snowman, they'd call, nudge me back,
silence cracking like a crocus—
the reveal, all that breaking, a kiss.
I don't know if I loved anything more.
When my father died, a backhoe broke
the sky open, which filled with crows,
and a dusting coated the cars lining
the cemetery road. Snow falling
on my father's death day, a little much
even for me, so prone to melancholy,
which is a way of skitching your loss.
Years ago, I had a friend, who used to say
love is a kind of opening.
She had a freezer stashed with vodka
and chocolate, a way of making me crash
on her couch. My friend was talking
about trees, what we know, what we feel,
how they conspire each other.
I was afraid my body would fly open,
a blizzard of wings, that if I gave up
grieving, he'd die all over again,
or I'd die without something to grieve.

She must've known this too,
how winter shuts a mouth down,
then more mouth, more mouth.
Some days, the light right,
I walk an hour or so into a stand of birches,
the space between trees, and it's like
the trees pass through me. Ghosts
of my breath, my father, my friend
sitting on the couch in her apartment—
All there. I hear them talking
and want to slip off my shoes—
Snow, listening, the nerve to stay awhile,
it's exactly like she was saying.

Acknowledgments

Bless my poetry friends and fellow readers who have abided these long years and saw this book through: Camille Dungy, Patrick Phillips, Michael Collier, Cate Marvin, Major Jackson, Nick Flynn, Matt Donovan, Debra Nystrom, C. Dale Young, Rick Barot, Elizabeth Scanlon, Ed Skoog, Bryan Walpert, Kevin Craft, Jeffrey McDaniel, Michael Bazzett, Paige Ackerson-Kiely and the litany of Davids: Baker, Biespiel, Hollander, Roderick, Sampliner. I am grateful to my teachers for their patience and fellow traveling, and to my collaborators, artistic and otherwise: Jonathan Lipkin, Chad Kinsey, Ben Neill, Jeff Geib, Joe Herskovitz, Sam Mustafa, Hugh Sheehy and G.

Heaps of gratitude for Bread Loaf and Sewanee Writers' Conferences, as well as the Virginia Center for Creative Arts and Gullkistan Center for Creativity for scholarships and residencies that have afforded time and focus. Thanks, too, to my people, students and colleagues at Ramapo College of New Jersey and Sarah Lawrence.

It's been a long time coming: Thank you to my family, my wife Marianne and my kids Aidan and Owen, for being way too dedicated, patient, fun, and loving. I am grateful for every door the Sullivan and Tyson families have kept open, for their love and meals. Blessed, too, for the friendships of the Stein-Marrisons, McCarthys, Drake-Hares.

Special thanks to James Long and everyone at LSU Press. It's good to have a home.

In some form or other, poems herein have appeared in other publications. I am grateful to the editors and readers of the following magazines and the dedication they bring: *Alaska Quarterly Review:* "Global Studies"; *American Poetry Review:* "Afghanistan," "Disgrace and Oblivion in Ancient Rome," "Elegy with a Landscape of Iceland by Georg Guðni," "Gainer," "Palouse," and "Sunflowers" (*Best American Poetry 2019*); *Blackbird:* "Puberty with Self-Portait as Tiffky Doofky"; *The Collagist:* "Leaving Well

Enough Alone"; *Colorado Review:* "The Pine Barrens: A Sermon"; *Columbia: A Journal of Art and Literature* (reprinted in *The Grief Diaries*): "Small Orange"; *Crab Orchard Review:* "The Ask"; *The Common:* "Advice to a Son as Garden Statuary"; *Kenyon Review:* "Elegy with Icarus and the Heart of a Hummingbird"; *Los Angeles Review:* "The Listening"; *New England Review:* "Landscape Resembling My Mother Dying" and "Self-Portrait as Last Pawn Shop in New Jersey"; *The New Republic:* "Recess"; *Poetry Northwest:* "Poem at the End of a Pier"; *Scoundrel Time:* "Prayer for That Little Exhaustion of Light"; *Thrush:* "Parking Garage" and "Polycardial"; *Tin House:* "Halo" and "This Drink Tastes like History"; and *Waxwing:* "Dedication" and "Primitivo Negativo."

Notes and Dedications

Just after September 11, 2001, my brother re-enlisted in the military. He was deployed in Afghanistan in 2003 and continues to serve.

"Dedication," for my boys, Aidan and Owen.

"Afghanistan," for my brother, Dolph.

"Disgrace and Oblivion in Ancient Rome" was inspired and informed by the work of Harriet Flowers, and references various historical sites in Lithuania, and is for my friends: Gabija, Judita, and the poet Kerry Shawn Keys.

"This Drink Tastes Like History" refers to the poet Larry Levis, the diving horses and "Diving Girls" of the Steel Pier in Atlantic City, the blizzard of 1996, the band SUPERNAG, the writer and sometime bartender Max Watman, and is in memory of my history teacher sometime bartender father.

"Landscape Resembling My Mother Dying" notes the Marathon Battery Factory in Cold Spring, New York, and mentions the strobe photography of Edgerton in the collection of the MIT Museum.

"Elegy with a Landscape of Iceland by Georg Guðni" is in memory of Chuck Kaiser, lover of life, and for his kids and Chad Kinsey. The poem makes reference to Silfra, Iceland, a rift in the divergent boundary between tectonic plates. Georg Guðni Hauksson (1961–2011) was a wonderful Icelandic painter.

"Elegy with Icarus and the Heart of a Hummingbird" is for Philipstown, New York.

"Palouse" refers to the geologically complex area covering parts of eastern Washington and Oregon. It's known for winter wheat and places like Walla Walla. Homage to Stan.

"Puberty with Self-Portrait as Tiffky Doofky" is for Alan Shapiro in conversation with his poem "Space Dog."

"Halo." In my early twenties, I worked and lived in a group home serving Native American youth. This same experience is referenced in "Self-Portrait as Last Pawn Shop in New Jersey."

"Global Studies," for my colleagues at Ramapo.

"Lithium Bath," for Michael Bazzett and the people of San Miguel de Allende.

"Primitivo Negativo," for Skoog, Genoways and Watman, and the good life.

"The Listening," for Catherine Barnett.

9 780807 174050